FAsD Is My SuPErpoweR

Helping Kids Understand the Strengths of Their Diagnosis

Emily Hargrove

Acknowledgment

Zaria Brown, for editing.

Jace Hargrove, for being a supportive husband.

ALC, for speaking words of wisdom.

God, for creating me with purpose.

Table of Content

HELLO, FRIEND! I'm Emily, and I'm thrilled that you've chosen this book with journal prompts to embark on a journey of discovering your strengths! I want you to know that I, too, have FASD and am constantly learning new things about myself just like you can. Before we begin, there are a few important things I want to share with you.

First, remember that you are here with a purpose. Never forget that! Second, I've provided some blank lines in this book just for you. Feel free to use these spaces to jot down your own thoughts. While I'll be addressing specific aspects of FASD, I won't cover everything. That's where you come in! FASD is unique to each individual, and your journey is exceptional. I have no doubt that your story is incredible!

Let this book serve as your guide as you explore FASD and discover the strengths within you.

Let's get started!

First off, what is FASD?

Excellent question! FASD stands for Fetal Alcohol Spectrum Disorder. This means that when you were developing as a baby, you were exposed to alcohol. Did you know that it's estimated that I in 20 children in a typical classroom has an FASD? This means you probably know other kids or have friends who share a similar experience. Just like you, I was exposed to alcohol during development, and I, too, face a few challenges. But here's the important part: that's okay... because many people, whether they have FASD or not, encounter difficulties in their lives, and we are not alone in this journey. I have friends and family who support and love me just the way I am!

Sometimes there are other related terms we can hear about FASD. Some of those are fetal alcohol syndrome (FAS), partial fetal alcohol syndrome (pFAS), prenatal exposure to alcohol (PAE), alcohol related neurodevelopmental disorder (ARND), and others. They are all similar although they have different names. You may even have a different diagnosis from the examples I gave. Feel free to write down your diagnosis. If you are unsure, that's ok! That's why FASD works just fine.

So what does this say about me?

It says that you were designed with a unique purpose to help those around you see the world differently.

You see, our brains and bodies do not work quite like everyone else. This can be frustrating to us sometimes. It can make us feel like we do not belong or do not fit in because we can work so hard at doing things like everyone else AND because our bodies work extra hard, it can make us feel tired! BUT, I know FASD heroes, and I look up to them. They are changemakers, and they work hard to show others how to have *COMPASSION, KINDNESS,* and *UNDERSTANDING* for those who may do things differently from others.

Can you think of ways you have been kind to others who may have been having a difficult time? (Take a minute to think about these questions and then answer)

____

____

____

Can you think of any "heroes" you can look up to as examples of people who show others how to be kind, compassionate, and understanding?

____

____

____

Write in your
superpowers
on the cape!

ALWAYS REMEMBER
YOU ARE BRAVER THAN YOU BELIEVE,
STRONGER THAN YOU SEEM,
SMARTER THAN YOU THINK,
AND LOVED MORE THAN YOU KNOW.

So my brain works extra hard, huh?

Yep! My friend put it this way: Think about a race. You have all the runners at the starting point ready to take off down the track. Everyone is wearing a backpack, but some people have weights in their backpack. We have a few extra weights in our backpack, and this makes it harder to keep up with everyone else in the race. Can you relate to this?

You know what is amazing about this? We may be running the race with extra weights, but we still get up every day and keep going! You know a good word for this: ***PERSISTENT!***

Can you think of ways you have been persistent? Write down some challenges you have faced, but kept going anyway?

____

____

____

____

If you need some ideas or examples, let me tell you a few challenges I face but keep going anyway: some days, my memory is not the best, and I can forget things. Can you relate? I can also get easily overwhelmed with tasks. Maybe school can become overwhelming. There can be a lot of noise, lights, smells, and instructions, and this can feel like a lot. Often, I have to work extra hard to know how to communicate and act. Feel free to talk to your parent or caregiver about these challenges and ways you keep going!

The brain is fascinating because it has many different areas that enable us to do a wide range of things every single day! Our brains work exceptionally hard to perform these tasks due to the changes that occurred during our development. Sometimes, it can be challenging to describe what this experience feels like. Use the brain model below to draw how you imagine your brain looks when it's hard at work.

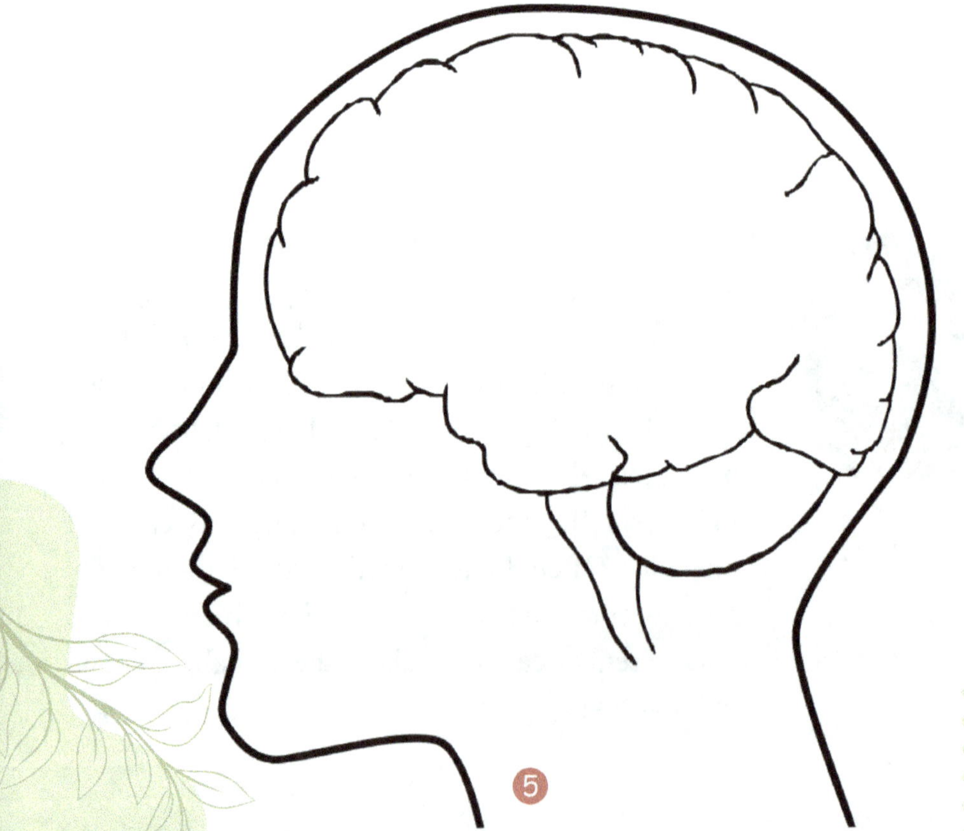

There are ways to support my brain?

Absolutely! Do you know another cool thing about the brain? You can strengthen it! Remember how my friend talked about running a race with extra weights in your backpack? Consider some of these ways to help you carry those extra weights!

Let's discuss four things that might work for you. Who knows? You may already be doing some of these.

1. Tasks with multiple steps can be overwhelming or difficult to remember. Write these steps down as a list, or have someone else do that for you. Give yourself permission to ask for help! Sometimes, we need someone to show us how to get started.

2. It may take more time than others to process information or to complete tasks. You can set aside extra time to complete projects, ask for more time in the classroom, or even remind your caregiver you may need more time to think about an answer to a question or solution to a problem.

3. In moments that feel overwhelming, have someone coach you through steps that can make things feel calmer. For example, there are breathing techniques and body scanning techniques that are easy to do and can be really helpful! Another example is seeking deep pressure in the form of a weighted blanket, a hug, or a cuddle from a pet.

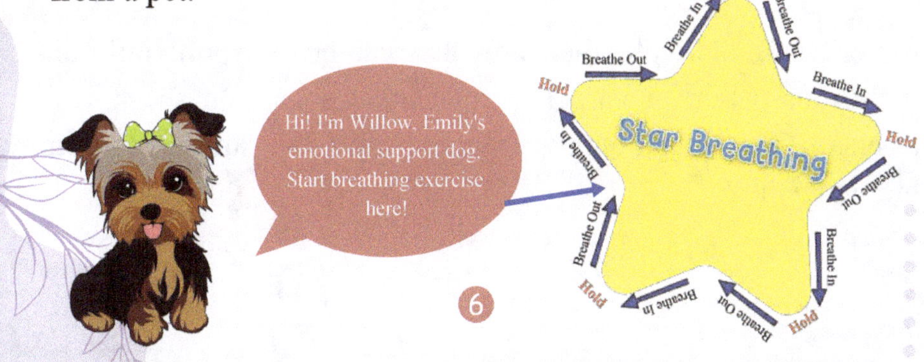

4. Try engaging in enriching activities or immerse yourself in an enriching environment! Did you know that learning to play the piano is a fantastic way to strengthen your brain? Anytime you use both hands simultaneously (that means at the same time) to do two different things, you're working to support your brain. Some more examples include learning the guitar, juggling, and practicing martial arts. These activities not only strengthen the brain but also boost self- confidence!

There are numerous ways to strengthen your brain. Perhaps you're already doing some of these things, or maybe you can think of other ways that haven't been mentioned. Maybe you play a musical instrument, excel in sports, have artistic talents, or enjoy writing. Just because our brains may work differently, it doesn't mean we can't excel in these areas or continue pursuing our talents and interests. Consider these things as strengths and powerful ways to enhance your brain!

Use this space to write down some of the ways you have been supporting your brain and/or what you would like to try.

Never be afraid to tell others how they can best support you! Talk with your parent or caregiver about ways you can speak with teachers, friends, and family about the ways you can support your brain together!

My body works extra hard, too?

Not only does your brain work extra hard, but your body does too. Nevertheless, you get up each morning and give it your best. You are a superhero!

FASD affects each of our bodies differently. In addition to the brain, it can also impact our heart, joints, or even our senses-like hearing. You might find it challenging to play sports or participate in activities in physical education because your body doesn't always cooperate. You may experience pain differently than someone else. Additionally, you might feel more overwhelmed or distracted by your senses. Just as our brains were influenced during development, so were our bodies. Understanding this can help you make sense of why some things are difficult and why some days are harder than others.

How can I support my body?

1. Be kind to yourself. Our bodies can tire easily, and there will be days when our energy is low, and that's perfectly okay!

2. Because we may not feel certain sensations like everyone else, we might miss a few things. For instance, we might not always feel pain. If you get hurt while playing, don't be afraid to tell someone, even if you don't feel pain. Another example is that we don't always feel hungry and may forget to eat. You can set up reminders to eat to best support your body!

3. Healthy sleep patterns are also good for our bodies. Do you know what healthy sleep looks like? Well, depending on your age, you should aim for anywhere from 8 to 13 hours of uninterrupted sleep each night. This means that when you go to bed, you should be able to fall asleep easily, and if you wake up, you should be able to go back to sleep without difficulty. We don't always do this very well. If you feel like your sleep isn't the best, talk to a parent or caregiver. Maybe you can work out ways to better support your sleep.

4. Communicate with your medical provider! From my experience, medical providers may not always connect our physical health challenges with our FASD diagnosis, but that's okay! You and your parent or caregiver have the power to educate your medical provider.

So, you're like a superhero, continuing to persevere even when you're tired or overwhelmed! I'm incredibly proud of you, and I know others are too. Use this space to jot down the ways you might experience your body working extra hard, yet you keep pushing forward!

You can even use this cartoon to draw an arrow pointing to or circle areas of your body where you might experience pain or discomfort.

You could be feeling that right now, such as a stomachache, or there might be something you feel more regularly or every day, like pain in your knees or a headache.

Feel free to share any of your aches or pains with your parent. And remember, you might not feel pain like everyone else, even after getting hurt. So, if you have any questions about how your body responds to pain, use this page to help you organize your thoughts and questions for a conversation with your caregiver.

So how can I tell my story?

I'm delighted you asked that question! Your story encompasses your diagnosis, your challenges, your strengths, and so much more! You are more than all of those things. In the beginning, I reminded you not to forget that you were created on purpose, with a purpose. Your story is beautiful and deserves to be shared. You never know who might need to hear your story or who you may inspire. It takes *BRAVERY* to share your story!

Talk to your parent or caregiver about your story and ways you can share your story in an encouraging way. Being a self-advocate takes *COURAGE!*

You were given this life for a reason! Use this space to write down all the things about your story that you find important and beautiful, and that may even help you better understand yourself. You might even want to draw or doodle to express your story.

Doodle Page

Telling your *SUPERHERO* story starts with better understanding yourself, and you are on that journey!

Sometimes along that journey, you may feel a bunch of emotions, and sometimes they may be hard to express, and that's ok! Use the blank faces to draw emotions you may feel but do not see listed.

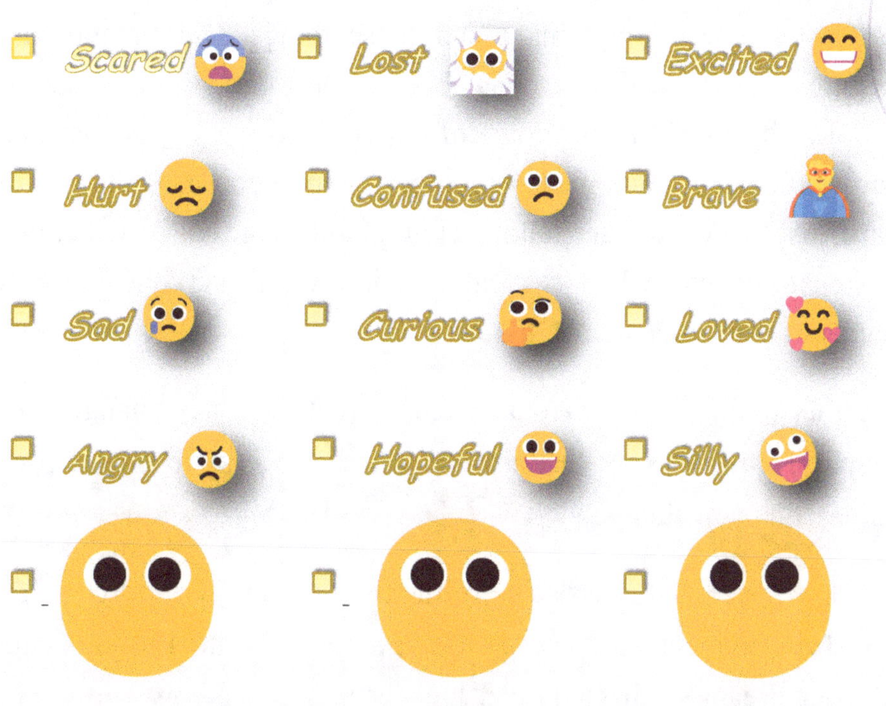

- Scared
- Lost
- Excited
- Hurt
- Confused
- Brave
- Sad
- Curious
- Loved
- Angry
- Hopeful
- Silly

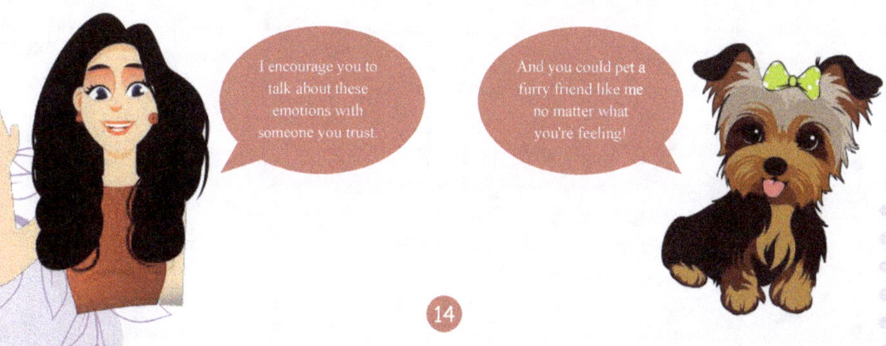

What does it mean to build a dream?

"The future belongs to those who believe in the beauty of their dreams" - Eleanor Roosevelt.

Sometimes, we think about what it will be like when we grow up. We might imagine what we'll do, who we'll meet, or the places we'll go. It's wonderful to think about these things. Our dreams can require *FAITH* and *PERSISTENCE.* One thing I know about people with FASD is that some of our superpowers are persistence and faith. Persistence means to keep going even when things are hard, just like we've been talking about. Faith is the ability to believe in something even when we cannot see it or when everyone else says it cannot happen or will be too hard.

Another thing to know about dreams is that they may change over time, and that's okay! Our dreams can evolve as we grow up or experience new things.

Use this space to discuss some of the things you want to do, people you'd like to meet, and places you'd like to go. Write down the date of your dream so that you can look back and see how you might change and grow over time.

____

____

____

____

____

MY DREAM

What does it mean to have goals?

A goal is a little different from a dream. A goal is something you take specific steps to achieve. Perhaps you want to set a goal to help make your dream come true. For instance, if you dream of earning a degree and using it at a university, a goal could be to do your best at school right now. You can write about the ways you want to excel at school, which might include some of the strategies we discussed earlier. Or perhaps you have goals related to learning more about your FASD or offering better support for FASD, or goals that involve highlighting the strengths of your FASD.

Please use the following to guide you as your write about your goals.

THE FIRST GOAL:

What I am doing now to reach this goal:

What else I can do to reach this goal:

THE SECOND GOAL:

What I am doing now to reach this goal:

What else I can do to reach this goal:

THE THIRD GOAL:

What I am doing now to reach this goal:

What else I can do to reach this goal:

We can have multiple goals. I want to encourage you to keep writing these goals and action steps down! Just because you ran out of space here in this journal, it does not mean you cannot keep doing it in another notebook. Here are a few extra lines to keep writing down your thoughts. Having goals is part of what makes you a superhero!

What about my faith?

This section is for those who find strength in their faith and through words of scripture. I understand that not everyone will relate to this section. Personally, I find a lot of strength in my faith, and maybe you can too. I just wanted to offer a few words of encouragement from the Bible that I find comforting. Feel free to write these down and place them where you can see them to be reminded of your strengths.

"For you formed my inward parts; you knitted me together in my mother's womb. I praise you, for I am fearfully and wonderfully made. Wonderful are your works; my soul knows it very well."

(Psalm 139:13-14)

"I chose you before I formed you in the womb; I set you apart before you were born."

(Jeremiah 1:5)

"The Lord is the One who will go before you. He will be with you; He will not leave you or forsake you. Do not be afraid or discouraged. "

(Deuteronomy 31:8)

"But He said to me, 'My grace is sufficient for you, for power is perfected in weakness.' Therefore, I will most gladly boast all the more about my weaknesses, so that Christ's power may reside in me. So I take pleasure in weaknesses, insults, catastrophes, persecutions, and in pressures, because of Christ. For when I am weak, then I am strong."

(2 Corinthians 12:9-10)

Many other scriptures and words of encouragement come to mind. Feel free to use the following area to write them down.

What does my future look like?

This is up to you, my superhero friend! What do I mean by that? Don't let anyone tell you that FASD is going to hold you back. Keep learning about yourself. Keep asking for help when needed. Keep using ways to support and strengthen your brain and body. Keep telling your story. Keep developing your dreams and goals. And, if you are like me, keep finding strength in your faith!

This is just the beginning! You are capable of changing the world around you by showing compassion, teaching understanding, and demonstrating bravery and persistence. You, my FASD Superhero, are one-of-a-kind!

Resources

We do not have to walk this journey alone! Please check out this list of helpful sources for FASD information and advocacy:

fasdunited.org

https://alcfasdchangemakers.org/

http://www.proofalliance.org/

EMILY
HARGROVE
CONSULTING

WHERE FAITH AND FASD COLLIDE

https://www.emilyhargrovefasdcounselingandconsulting.com/

FASD Heroes

On the next page, you will see just a few of the FASD Superheroes who have made a difference in my life. Each person below has FASD and inspire me to keep pushing! They are from all over the world. I encourage you to find your FASD heroes, and to continue to be the superhero you already are!

Each hero is from an international group known as the Adult Leadership Collaborative of the FASD Changemakers. You can call us ALC for short. They represent men and women all over the globe from all walks of life who all live and thrive with FASD. They, like you and me, have unique challenges and unique strengths. Some are moms. Some are dads. Some are gifted speakers and teachers. Some are fantastic at writing, art, and photography. Others are gifted in lifting others up (both literally with their big muscles and figuratively with their big hearts). Some received their diagnosis at young ages, while others did not receive theirs until they were adults. Their stories and perspectives have shaped the way the world sees FASD for the better. They aren't afraid to share their story, because they know it can and will make a difference, even for the person reading this book! They are superheroes.

Anique Lutke

Byron Jones

CJ Lutke

Kat Griffin

Gina Schumaker

Jessica Birch

Jacob Dedman

Maggie May

Justin Shepherd

Kim Doktor

Justin Mitchell

Myles Himmelreich

Tonje Hognerud

Shannon Butt

Nury Van Beers

About the Author

Emily Hargrove was diagnosed with fetal alcohol syndrome (FAS) at the age of one, receiving a life-long, full-body diagnosis from Vanderbilt Clinic. Despite a grim prognosis from doctors, who believed she would likely never succeed in school, Emily drew strength from her faith, believing that God always has something bigger in store for each of us. She decided to become more than a statistic and now uses her voice to empower others who have felt disenfranchised, leveraging her God-given love of learning to research the very condition with which she has been diagnosed.

As a member of the International Adult Leadership Collaborative of the FASD Changemakers (ALC), Emily partners with changemakers across the globe to strengthen the voices of adults with fetal alcohol spectrum disorder (FASD) and create inclusive environments while mitigating stigma. In 2020, she co-authored an article published in the Routledge Handbook of Social Work and Addictive Behaviors on the chronic healthcare implications of adults with FASD.

Since 2008, Emily has traveled as an educator, self-advocate, and speaker, sharing her personal story of adoption, faith, FASD, and resilience, as well as her research. She is a founding member of Self-Advocates with an FASD in Action (SAFA) and a former expert panel member for SAMHSA's FASD Center for Excellence. Emily has also partnered with state affiliates of FASD United and the Arc of the United States, developing and facilitating presentations and training for various audiences.

Currently, Emily is partnering with the University of Rochester and fellow ALC members to develop an app aimed at helping adults with FASD manage their health. The ALC's second study on FASD and quality of life is currently being published in the peer-reviewed journal, Disabilities. She is also the board president of the FASD Collaborative Project.

Emily graduated Summa Cum Laude with a Bachelor's in Psychology and Counseling, minoring in Christian Ministries (B.S.). She holds a Master's of Philosophy in Psychology (M.Phil.) and is currently a Doctor of Philosophy in Psychology (Ph.D.) candidate with a dissertation focus on FASD and spiritual development. For five years, she volunteered at a family crisis center as a mentor and group facilitator. Emily is a certified affiliate and member of the American Philosophical Practitioner Association (APPA) as a philosophical counselor.

For seven years, Emily and her husband Jace served as youth pastors, igniting the fire within their students. She has a love for the Spanish language and a heart for the people of Mexico, having returned to the same village on mission trips for many years. Emily also serves on a local Miss America Scholarship Pageant board, guiding young women to lead through fostering interview skills, resume building, and instilling the value of service.

In her spare time, when she is not working on her dissertation or chasing her two-year-old, Emily enjoys studying complementary and alternative approaches to well-being. This passion is reflected in her professional work as a chiropractic assistant/massage therapist, her interest in Native American/holistic remedies, and her pursuit of philosophy as a mode of healing. She also enjoys playing classical piano and the Native American flute, and being outdoors, particularly horseback riding, which she developed a love for growing up on a farm. Emily and her husband are expecting their second child in September of 2024.

Emily is the owner of Emily Hargrove Consulting Where Faith and FASD Collide. EHC offers philosophical counseling sessions, speaking services, and FASD inspired clothing.

For more information check out:

http://www.emilyhargrovefasdcounselingandconsulting.com/

This book is dedicated to all the FASD Superheroes everywhere.